Cybersecurity
Analyst

Other titles in the *Cutting Edge Careers* series include:

Big Data Analyst

Robotics Engineer

Software Engineer

Video Game Designer

Virtual Reality Developer

Cybersecurity Analyst

Melissa Abramovitz

ReferencePoint Press®

San Diego, CA

© 2018 ReferencePoint Press, Inc.
Printed in the United States

For more information, contact:
ReferencePoint Press, Inc.
PO Box 27779
San Diego, CA 92198
www.ReferencePointPress.com

Picture credits:
Cover: iStockphoto/Baranozdemir
 6: Maury Aaseng
15: Associated Press
29: Thinkstock Images
41: Associated Press
48: Associated Press

LIBRARY OF CONGRESS CATALOGING-IN-PUBLICATION DATA

Name: Abramovitz, Melissa, 1954– author.
Title: Cybersecurity Analyst/by Melissa Abramovitz.
Description: San Diego, CA: ReferencePoint Press, Inc., 2018. | Series: Cutting Edge Careers | Audience: Grades 9 to 12. | Includes bibliographical references and index.
Identifiers: LCCN 2017001818 (print) | LCCN 2017010096 (ebook) | ISBN 9781682821824 (hardback) | ISBN 9781682821831 (eBook)
Subjects: LCSH: Computer networks—Security measures—Vocational guidance—Juvenile literature.
Classification: LCC TK5105.59 .A245 2018 (print) | LCC TK5105.59 (ebook) | DDC 005.8023--dc23
LC record available at https://lccn.loc.gov/2017001818

CONTENTS

CYBERSECURITY ANALYST AT A GLANCE

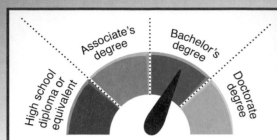

Minimum Educational Requirements

High school diploma or equivalent · Associate's degree · Bachelor's degree · Doctorate degree

Personal Qualities

- ☑ Detail oriented
- ☑ Creativity
- ☑ Technical skills
- ☑ Analytical skills
- ☑ Problem-solving skills

Working Conditions

Indoors

Pay

$60,000 ⟷ $250,000

82,900
In the United States in 2014

1,000,000
Unfilled jobs worldwide

Number of Jobs

Growth projected by US Bureau of Labor Statistics between 2014–2018

18%

Future Job Outlook: *EXCELLENT*

Source: Bureau of Labor Statistics, *Occupational Outlook Handbook*. www.bls.gov

The Need for Cybersecurity Analysts

As cyberattacks on computers and other digital devices have proliferated worldwide, so too has the need for cybersecurity analysts. Each year more and more people use the Internet for shopping, entertainment, communication, and other pursuits. With every new user and account created, the number and sophistication of cyberpredators and hackers—people who gain unauthorized access to and steal digital data—rises dramatically.

Most people are only aware of major breaches that affect large companies. However, experts note that tens of thousands of minor security breaches occur each day, though few companies report them. A 2015 report by the cybersecurity company Symantec highlights the vast number of unreported cyber intrusions. Although the reported number of identities exposed by cybercriminals in 2015 was 429 million, Symantec estimates the actual number is closer to 500 million.

Making matters worse, many organizations and individuals don't even know they have been hacked. As P.W. Singer and Allan Friedman of the Brookings Institution note in their book *Cybersecurity and Cyberwar*, 97 percent of all Fortune 500 companies had been hacked by 2014, "and 3 percent likely have been too and just don't know it."[1]

Factors That Drive Cybercrime

Numerous trends, including the proliferation of smartphones and the Internet of Things (IoT), are driving the increase in cybercrime. Hackers increasingly target IoT devices like web-enabled baby monitors, online refrigerators, and "smart" lighting controls and cameras because these devices have certain kinds of applications

Technology and Human Factors

For many years, cybersecurity professionals used firewalls and other anti-malware tools to protect computer systems from outside attacks. But more recently they have shifted their focus. Research indicates company insiders or trusted contractors are responsible for many breaches—some accidentally and some on purpose. Therefore, cybersecurity analysts have started to focus more on the "human factors" involved in cyberattacks.

A 2015 study by the British technology firm Loudhouse found that insiders contribute to 58 percent of cybersecurity breaches, and 82 percent of these result from unintentional actions. For example, an employee might introduce malware to a personal device by clicking on a phishing e-mail, which might appear to be from a trusted friend. Or he or she may plug a USB device that has been contaminated with malware into a networked computer. Because such mistakes can cost millions, organizations are increasingly investing in education programs that teach employees to be wary of such schemes. These programs are among the most effective ways to prevent such breaches.

Breaches that are perpetrated on purpose by insiders are harder to avoid and detect, since such people often have regular access to protected data and know about existing security features. A well-known deliberate insider breach occurred in 2013 when Edward Snowden, a disgruntled employee who worked for National Security Agency (NSA) contractor Booz Allen, leaked hundreds of thousands of classified documents. He did so by smuggling data out of the organization on a USB drive and giving it to reporters and the hacktivist organization WikiLeaks. The damage to national security was significant, and cybersecurity analysts continue to search for the best ways to thwart insiders like Snowden.

that weaken their security. For example, smart watches have an application that allows users to transmit information collected by the watch to another party, which weakens security. A study conducted by the technology company Hewlett-Packard in 2015 found that it also allows 90 percent of these transmissions to be intercepted. In addition, IoT devices come with factory-set passwords; these represent another security weakness, as many owners never bother to change the passwords the equipment comes with, which are then easily hacked.

An attack that occurred in October 2016 demonstrated the dangers associated with factory-set passwords. Hackers breached thousands of IoT devices using Mirai malware (malicious software), which scans for default passwords. When the malware encountered a default password, the hackers used it to take control of the device, and in doing so turned all the devices into what is known as a zombie army, or botnet. The botnet executed the attackers' commands to flood certain websites with so much cybertraffic that the sites temporarily shut down. This resulted in what is called a distributed denial of service (DDoS) that affected numerous websites, including Amazon and Twitter.

The growing use of cloud and other third-party contractors also fuels cybercrime. The cloud consists of online locations used to store data outside a given computer network. Contractors are people or companies who are hired by another company for specific purposes. Contractors are often given access to the hiring company's computer networks. Since many contractors' systems have lax security, criminals exploit these weaknesses to breach the hiring company's databases. Indeed, according to a 2016 Soha Systems survey, 63 percent of data breaches involve third-party network access. In one major 2015 breach, hackers stole personal information about millions of federal employees from the US Office of Personnel Management. They gained access to the information through a subcontractor called KeyPoint Government Solutions.

> "Virtually every national security threat and crime problem the FBI faces is cyber-based or facilitated."[2]
>
> —FBI director James B. Comey

Another driver of cybercrime is people who inadvertently make themselves victims. Many social media users tend to overshare information about themselves, some of it very personal. Some details—such as birth dates or the name of one's school— essentially end up giving criminals a road map to individuals' passwords and habits.

Finally, hackers persist because they rarely get caught or punished. Many operate long-distance, from areas in which law enforcement is weak or nonexistent. They use technologies like the dark web and TOR software, which conceal their identities and locations by utilizing areas of cyberspace outside the Internet. Then, as soon as cybersecurity and law enforcement experts figure out how to neutralize or track cybercriminals, the criminals create new ways to hack and hide. This makes catching and punishing them an uphill battle.

Why Is Cybersecurity Important?

Cybercriminals have financial, political, social, and personal motivations. Their attacks damage millions of individuals, organizations, and even entire countries. Hackers empty people's bank accounts, use or sell their credit card numbers, and steal their identities. They shut down critical services, such as electric power distribution or water service. They could endanger lives by remotely reprogramming networked medical devices like intravenous pumps and cause them to, say, deliver lethal doses of medication. Nation-states hire cybercriminals for political purposes, such as when Russian hackers breached the Democratic Party's computers to allegedly influence the 2016 US presidential election. Terrorists use cyberspace to plan and wage war or to steal secret information, which makes cybersecurity a national security issue. As FBI director James B. Comey told the US Congress in February 2016, "Virtually every national security threat and crime problem the FBI faces is cyber-based or facilitated."[2]

According to the cybersecurity professional organization ISACA, in 2016 cybersecurity breaches around the world cost more than $618 billion. Each breach costs an organization an average of $3.79 million. These factors, and the damage that cybercriminals leave in their wake, underlie the need for an increasing number of cybersecurity professionals.

Changing Strategies

A January 2016 survey performed by ISACA found that most cybersecurity professionals believe the top cyberthreats stem from social engineering (hackers who exploit human weaknesses); insider threats (that is, employees, ex-employees, and trusted contractors who have access to digital systems); and advanced persistent threats (APTs), which are cyberattacks launched by well-coordinated teams of cybercriminals who exploit human and technical security weaknesses. "Hackers are no longer breaking in through back doors which may trigger alarms," explains cybersecurity expert Spencer Coursen. "Today they are stealing the keys of authorized users and walking right through the front door."[3]

As the strategies and methods used by cybercriminals change, so too must those used by cybersecurity professionals to fight them. Such strategies have shifted from simply blocking malware to using security teams that address all the relevant factors, including what are known as "human factors"—the actions or errors of people who open the door to cybercriminal activity. This shifting focus requires cybersecurity professionals to set new goals, as they strive "to be able to move from reacting to such attacks after the fact to operationally preventing such attacks,"[4] as Comey puts it.

However, these changes have vastly broadened the range of cybersecurity jobs. Consider that until around 2010, few specific cybersecurity roles existed; one or two security people typically occupied a small corner in an organization's information technology (IT) department. Today, however, there is a growing need for analysts and engineers who specialize in various aspects of prevention, detection, mitigation, and recovery.

A Growing Need

The need for specialized security professionals goes hand in hand with the general demand for more of them. Indeed, cybersecurity is one of the technology-related professions that has more job openings than qualified people to fill them. For example, in late 2016 the US Department of Homeland Security (DHS) announced that there were more than half a million job openings for IT professionals, including those in cybersecurity. A 2015 report by the cybersecurity service company Cisco similarly indicated that there were more than 1 million unfilled cybersecurity jobs worldwide. Despite these opportunities, the limited supply of qualified individuals makes it difficult to meet this demand.

Government agencies and other potential employers are thus promoting cybersecurity-related classes and internships to interest middle and high school students in these careers. For example, in 2013 the Northrop Grumman corporation began offering internships for students aged sixteen and older to help meet its need for more than seven hundred new cybersecurity professionals over the next several years.

The trend toward establishing cybersecurity departments with a range of experts in large organizations was exemplified by the fact that in September 2016, the White House hired its first federal chief information security officer (CISO). As the first person to serve in this position, Brigadier General (retired) Gregory J. Touhill oversees a nationwide initiative to strengthen all aspects of cybersecurity. Part of his job includes launching an initiative to hire more security professionals. As Tony Scott and J. Michael Daniel, White House press officers, put it, "Strong cybersecurity depends on robust policies, secure networks and systems and, importantly, a cadre of highly skilled cybersecurity talent."[5]

CHAPTER 1

What Does a Cybersecurity Analyst Do?

Cybersecurity analysts do a lot of important work. At its core, the job involves using what is known as a "threat-based approach" to determine which digital information in a computer network needs protecting, which defenses should be used to protect it, and what should be done when these defenses are breached. Part of the job is also to find "bugs," or vulnerabilities, in computer code; design and produce cybersecurity tools; troubleshoot cyberattacks; and work with other IT specialists, like computer engineers, to develop and implement company-wide security policies and processes.

For example, consider a cybersecurity analyst job advertised by aerospace contractor Lockheed Martin in December 2016. Lockheed was searching for someone who could help detect, identify, and analyze threats to company systems; support the company's cyber incident response team; develop ways to prevent and mitigate cyberattacks; perform forensic analyses when breaches occur; deliver threat analysis briefings; and create incident reports. These duties fit with analysts' overall responsibility for analyzing and addressing multiple risks that threaten cybersecurity.

Most cyberattacks result from what are known as stacked risks—combinations of smaller risks that add up to huge security gaps. For instance, the 2013 Target breach, in which hackers stole 70 million customers' credit and debit card information, likely resulted from about fifty individual security gaps. These gaps included giving outside contractors direct access to company databases and the fact that Target lacked a formal cyberthreat response plan. It is a cybersecurity analyst's job to protect against these stacked risks, among other things.

Defense-in-Depth Strategies

Defense-in-depth strategies address the virtual, physical, and human elements that come together in cyberspace. They involve putting up hardware and software barriers to defend computer networks from virtual elements, such as people who use the Internet, Internet servers, and providers like cloud companies. They also involve protecting physical devices like printers and routers from tampering (by restricting access to them). Finally, they involve addressing human factors, which means understanding who poses a threat, what they seek to achieve, and which insiders may accidently or purposely help them.

Strategies to address human factors include diminishing the chances that someone will deliberately commit an insider crime. This can mean enhancing employee satisfaction and loyalty, often by building a culture that makes employees feel valued. Decreasing an insider's chance of accidentally causing a breach mostly involves improving employees' cybersecurity awareness and offering training to spot scams, follow disaster recovery plans, and look out for criminals who may try to manipulate insiders. In one such program at Lockheed Martin, security employees send other employees tempting web links to test how much they have learned from their cyber education programs. Any employee who clicks on such a link is immediately required to take a cybersecurity awareness class.

Combatting Real-World Threats

This threat-based approach evolved after the turn of the twenty-first century, when experts realized that it was not working to simply respond to hacks after they occurred. So they adopted threat-based cybersecurity, which is sometimes also called a Red Team approach. It involves teams of ethical hackers who work together to break in to computer networks to reveal their technical and human weaknesses (a technique known as penetration testing). These analysts also determine how and why a particular organization is likely to face certain threats. They also simulate ways in which these threats are likely to present themselves, and how they might respond to the analysts' mitigation strategies.

It is important to distinguish malicious, or black-hat, hackers from ethical, or white-hat, hackers. Black hats are criminals who seek to exploit security vulnerabilities for their own gain; white hats are cybersecurity analysts who seek to protect such vulnerabilities. Billy Rios is a white-hat hacker who uses his skills to promote public safety. Rios was one of the first experts to expose vulnerabilities in medical devices like hospital infusion pumps after a penetration-testing job at the Mayo Clinic in 2013 made him aware of these problems. He sent the US Food and Drug Administration and device manufacturers videos and computer code he wrote to make them aware of the problem but was ignored for several years. Then, finally, in 2015 the US government realized that the dangers exposed by Rios and other analysts were very real, and officials urged manufacturers to improve device security.

A US government cybersecurity analyst monitors the nation's power grid and water and communications systems for unwanted cyberactivity. This is just one of the jobs that cybersecurity analysts do.

The CIA Triad and Defense-in-Depth Strategy

Threat-based cybersecurity is guided by a model called the CIA Triad. The letter *C* stands for confidentiality—keeping personal data and other valuable information private. The letter *I* stands for integrity—ensuring that a system is not changed without authorization. *A* stands for availability—ensuring that the system can be used as it is designed to be used. Analysts have several tools at their disposal to achieve CIA. Examples include encryption, which involves scrambling data; using firewalls, which block certain types of digital data; access control, which blocks unauthorized people from accessing a network; intrusion detection software, which detects unauthorized network use; and anti-malware software, which protects against malicious software. A newer type of intrusion-detection software—called machine-learning analytic software—is proving to be especially good at protecting cybernetworks. It alerts analysts to suspicious digital traffic that typically signifies the presence of malware and other criminal tools.

However, experts note that achieving security is a balancing act. Upholding confidentiality, integrity, and availability must be done in a way that also makes networks convenient, operable, and profitable. "If your data security is too restrictive, your flexibility and ability to conduct business will be negatively affected," explains network architect Kirk Steinklauber. "On the other hand, if your security is too lenient, you might be making it easier for potential intruders to find a backdoor."[6]

Finding the right balance also involves following what is known as a defense-in-depth strategy. This is an extension of the threat-based model that uses layers of security that each address specific vulnerabilities. Layering deters intruders because it forces

> "If your data security is too restrictive, your flexibility and ability to conduct business will be negatively affected. On the other hand, if your security is too lenient, you might be making it easier for potential intruders to find a backdoor."[6]
>
> —Network architect Kirk Steinklauber

them to penetrate many control levels to reach their target. Such layers feature defenses against all of the technical and human vulnerabilities that can weaken security, which include the connectivity of the Internet, malware, and the people who use computer systems. Until 2013 security analysts focused mostly on strengthening the layers that involve technical vulnerabilities. But numerous large breaches highlighted the importance of human vulnerabilities, and the focus shifted to addressing the human factors layers. "The reality is the weakest link within organizations is people," states Columbia Bank Audit and Risk Management Leader Scott Newman. "So, if your security awareness programs are not up to snuff, if they're not robust, if they're not focused on people, you're going to lose in the end."[7]

A Cybersecurity Tool

Cybersecurity experts are very concerned about how easily hackers can breach hospitals' cybernetworks and networked medical devices like intravenous pumps or X-ray machines. The fear is that they could be programmed to deliver lethal doses of medication or radiation, or used to hold patients hostage to ransom demands.

In 2014 the TrapX Security company launched a new tool to track this type of threat. The company created replicas of cybernetworks and Internet-connected hospital devices at more than sixty hospitals to use as bait for cyberattackers. The replicas looked real to Internet users, but TrapX used special software to detect and monitor intrusions. Over six months, hackers breached every single fake network and installed malware using a variety of techniques. Often, they used phishing ploys like making employees think e-mails came from a trusted source to lure these individuals into opening infected e-mails. Other hackers found and exploited digital holes in outdated software to steal patients' medical records to sell to other criminals. TrapX analysts traced many of the hackers to an eastern European server that cybercriminals are known to use.

Cybersecurity Analysis Jobs

Analyzing and implementing defense-in-depth cybersecurity is complex and requires many highly specialized skills. As a result, qualified cybersecurity analysts are in high demand. However, not all such positions contain the word *analyst*, and not all cybersecurity experts do the same thing. For instance, jobs in this category include penetration testers, cybersecurity architects, cybersecurity managers, network analysts, and threat analysts. In addition to being hired to do one of these specialized jobs, an analyst may also be expected to serve in multiple roles. One analyst may evaluate online traffic, look for security gaps, and perform penetration testing; another may design and implement security governance processes or analyze employee behavior and risk factors.

The range and depth of jobs also varies among organizations. For instance, government intelligence and law enforcement agencies use analysts to gather information and disrupt terrorists' online activities. An example of such work comes from a project dubbed Operation Cupcake that was undertaken by MI6, the British intelligence agency. MI6 analysts infiltrated an online magazine published by the terrorist group al Qaeda called *Inspire* magazine. Once in, they replaced an article on making homemade bombs with cupcake recipes. Intelligence agencies also hire digital forensic analysts to determine how a cyberattack occurred, who orchestrated it, what information was lost, and how the perpetrators can be found and arrested.

> "Looking to get into a career in cybersecurity analysis is quite challenging because the goalposts keep moving."[9]
>
> —Cyber Simplicity Ltd. director Raef Meeuwisse

Some analysts work for companies that develop, test, and sell tools that other cybersecurity analysts use. For example, the company CrowdStrike makes the Falcon security platform, which specializes in tracking, analyzing, and stopping cyberthreats. Cybersecurity platforms like Falcon are collections of tools that address all layers of defense-in-depth programs. CrowdStrike cofounder George Kurtz describes Falcon as "a neighborhood watch program on steroids."[8] One Falcon tool—called Falcon

Host—tracks, maps, graphs, and compares approximately 14 billion cyber events each day. It also blocks malware by learning to recognize new cyberthreat patterns.

However, since the cybersecurity discipline is changing so rapidly, analysts' tools and even their jobs are constantly evolving too. "Looking to get into a career in cybersecurity analysis is quite challenging because the goalposts keep moving," says cybersecurity expert Raef Meeuwisse, director of the British cybersecurity consulting company Cyber Simplicity Ltd. "There are a lot of very specific roles at present—but the nature, content, and objectives of those roles are subject to constant evolution."[9]

CHAPTER 2

How Do You Become a Cybersecurity Analyst?

Different organizations that hire cybersecurity analysts have varying requirements for the job, but most require at least a bachelor's degree and hands-on experience in computer science or a related field. The specific requirements are changing as the profession evolves, but the need for up-to-date technological knowledge and experience remain constant.

STEM Classes and More

The journey toward a career in cybersecurity analysis can start in middle and high school by taking science, technology, engineering, and mathematics (STEM) related classes. In addition to taking classes like algebra, geometry, chemistry, and physics, it helps to take computer-related classes like coding or web design.

The need for cybersecurity professionals has led numerous government agencies and private businesses to support STEM education at the high school level. For example, in 2016, the FBI partnered with Indiana University of Pennsylvania and several Pennsylvania school districts to launch the Model Cybersecurity Program. The program augments high school STEM courses and allows the FBI to educate students "before they make their life choices—to plant that seed that this is a potential career pathway,"[10] as FBI Supervisory Special Agent Christopher Geary puts it. Students can receive college credits for taking the classes, which address cybersecurity threats, data loss prevention, related laws, and more. Other programs, like Virginia's STEM Academy for middle and high school students, place students in internships with local businesses to give them hands-on training in general IT and specialized cybersecurity skills.

Although real-world experience and STEM classes help students prepare for a cybersecurity career, many teachers and industry experts say it is equally important to take classes that enhance creative thinking and problem solving. "[Students] don't have problem solving skills, and problem solving is computer science,"[11] says University of Maryland computer science professor

The National Youth Cyber Education Program

Students can gain firsthand cybersecurity knowledge and skills through the National Youth Cyber Education Program. This program, which is run by the US Air Force, puts on the CyberPatriot competition, cybercamps for middle and high school students, and a classroom-based Elementary School Cyber Education Initiative. The goal of these programs is to interest students in the field of cybersecurity at a young age.

The CyberPatriot competition challenges teams of middle and high school students to find and counteract cybersecurity vulnerabilities. They must do so without disrupting critical operations in models of virtual systems that are provided by actual companies. Teams can compete regionally, statewide, and nationally. Winners earn scholarship money and national honors. It also gives them the opportunity to access internships, mentoring, and cybersecurity jobs with sponsoring companies like Northrop Grumman.

Team coaches and participants are big fans of the competition. Coach Amy King of Douglas MacArthur High School states that along with learning about teamwork, planning, and leadership, her students "gained an understanding of the grave threat our society faces from cyber attack, and many of them have decided to make computer science or cyber security their focus in college." One high school student named Anthony went on to become a network analyst and engineer for a cybersecurity company. He called the competition "an amazing experience that can change someone's life" and noted that it was "ultimately the reason I hold my current career."

Quoted in CyberPatriot, "What Our Participants Are Saying." www.uscyberpatriot.org.

Marie des Jardins. She thinks that elementary, middle, and high schools should do more to enhance these skills. In addition, surveys conducted by the K–12 Cyber Security Education Think Tank found that college professors who teach cybersecurity courses think that high school classes that enhance writing and other communications skills are as important as STEM classes.

Many schools also have computer clubs or cybersecurity-related teams that provide valuable problem-solving experience. Most teams compete in events that take place at physical locations, but the High School Capture the Flag (HSCTF) competition, designed and run by students in the West Windsor–Plainsboro High School computer science club, occurs online. In this event, teams of students compete for cash prizes by capturing digital "flags" that are hidden or encrypted on online servers, using techniques like reverse engineering, code-breaking, hacking, and algorithm design.

Higher Education

Majoring in technology subjects in college can also help students prepare for a career in cybersecurity, though other majors may also lead to this path if the individual earns a bachelor's or master's degree. The Cyber Seek website, which provides a snapshot of cybersecurity jobs in the United States, revealed in late 2016 that 55 percent of employers wanted applicants for entry-level incident analyst/responder positions to have a bachelor's degree; 30 percent wanted them to have a graduate degree; and 15 percent requested a sub-bachelor's degree like an associate's degree. For mid-level information security analyst jobs, 63 percent wanted applicants to have a bachelor's degree, 34 percent a graduate degree, and 3 percent a sub-bachelor's degree.

The demand for analysts who have college degrees has led many colleges, universities, and technical schools to establish cybersecurity degree programs. Some of these degrees can be earned online. For example, Maryville University in St. Louis, Missouri, offers online bachelor of science and master of science programs in cybersecurity. Other schools offer multiple specialized degrees. For example, Utica College in Utica, New York, offers

Education and Internship Opportunities

There are a variety of education and internship programs that offer middle and high school students firsthand insight into what it's like to work in cybersecurity. For example, the GenCyber Academy of Excellence, funded by the National Security Agency and the National Science Foundation, offers summer programs at numerous colleges and universities throughout the United States.

One such program is at the Center for Cyber Security, which is housed at the University of San Diego. It gives high school students and computer science teachers opportunities to study computer networking, software engineering, forensics, and cyberdefenses. Participants also visit technology companies like Qualcomm and the Space and Naval Warfare Systems Command to learn about cybersecurity at these facilities. Those who attended the 2016 program raved about their experience. "It's been fantastic," said a high school student named Kellen. "It's actually exceeded my expectations." What high school teacher Dadre Rudolph learned from college-level instructors and industry professionals was extremely valuable. "I already do programming, but it was really great to hear from a top program what types of programs are used in the security world," she said. "It's very helpful as a new computer science teacher to hear what professionals in the field say."

Quoted in Gary Warth, "Next Generation Prepares for Digital Battle," *San Diego Union-Tribune*, July 29, 2016. www.sandiegouniontribune.com.

bachelor of science degrees in cybersecurity/cyber operations and cybersecurity/cybercrime and fraud investigation. It also offers a master of science degree in cybersecurity/computer forensics and cybersecurity/malware analysis, as well as a master of business administration (MBA) in cybersecurity.

The NSA and DHS have designated certain schools, such as Boston University and Ohio State University, as National Centers of Academic Assurance/Cyber Defense. Students who attend these schools may apply for scholarships and grants through the US Department of Defense Information Assurance Scholarship Program and the Scholarship for Service Program. This is another consideration to keep in mind when selecting a degree program.

Cybersecurity Certifications

Another way to enter this field is by earning a professional certification. Some, like the Certified Information Systems Security Professional (CISSP), cover general security analysis expertise. Others, like those that certify one's proficiency in network penetration testing, reflect expertise and training in narrower subfields.

Several international organizations offer certifications and training programs in this area. For example, the SANS Institute, which partners with the Global Information Assurance Certification (GIAC) program, offers the GIAC Certified Intrusion Analyst (GCIA) and the GIAC Certified Forensic Analyst (GCFA). Another reputable certifying organization is ISACA, which offers the Certified Information Systems Auditor (CISA), the Certified Information Security Manager (CISM), and the CISSP, among others.

> "If you are lacking a college education but have a leg up in cybersecurity training, then you can still snag a job."[17]
>
> —Cybersecurity Ventures CEO Steve Morgan

The International Information Systems Security Certification Consortium (ISC)[2] is another well-known certifying organization whose certifications include the CISSP and the Certified Cloud Security Professional (CCSP). These organizations offer online and in-person classes that help candidates prepare for certification exams. Prerequisites for taking these exams vary widely; for instance, candidates for some certifications are not required to attend training sessions. On the other hand, CISSP candidates must have a minimum of five years' experience in a paid cybersecurity job to take the exam.

The number and nature of cybersecurity certifications are evolving as the profession expands. For instance, in May 2016 GIAC announced that it was offering a new certification called the GPYC. It is for coders who use the Python programming language to create penetration testing tools. "Penetration testers can no longer wait for someone else to develop the tools they need and must know how to develop their own tools,"[12] says SANS Institute training course developer Mark Baggett of the GPYC.

The Value of Certifications

Cybersecurity certifications are becoming more important—employers are increasingly relying on them to make hiring and salary decisions. Indeed, a January 2016 ISACA survey of cybersecurity hiring managers revealed that 81 percent consider job applicants' certifications when they make selections and appointments. One such manager is Brent Deterding at the information security company LURHQ. "LURHQ requires all analysts to hold GIAC Intrusion Analyst certifications (GCIA)—and we tie this to promotions and additional salary," he says. "As a Security Operations Center Manager I have additional confidence in my team's abilities because they hold GIAC certifications."[13]

> "Certifications are great . . . but real knowledge and experience is better."[18]
>
> —Billy Rios, founder of the cybersecurity company WhiteScope

Many professionals attest to the value of certifications in enhancing their skills, confidence, and even the respect they get from their peers. "The intensive GIAC certification process has garnered me the respect of my boss and peers,"[14] states Matt Carpenter of Enterprise Information Systems. Security Manager Linda Dawson notes, "The CISM certification has helped me from the vice president level down to the frontline IT level. The knowledge I have is applicable globally, across multiple countries."[15] Another advantage, states cybersecurity consultant Marcello Melro, is that his CISM "brings credibility to the company [that] I am working for."[16]

In addition, although most employers favor job candidates with college degrees, some waive this requirement for certified professionals with proven experience and expertise. "If you are lacking a college education but have a leg up in cybersecurity training, then you can still snag a job,"[17] explains Cybersecurity Ventures CEO Steve Morgan.

However, some analysts question the value of certifications. Billy Rios, founder of the WhiteScope cybersecurity company, for example, states that "certifications are great . . . but real knowledge and experience is better."[18] A survey conducted by the National Research Council of the National Academies also found that some employers think that certifications restrict job candidates' problem-solving abilities. "A few [cybersecurity professionals] said that they sometimes omitted listing them on their resumes for this reason,"[19] the survey noted. However, most analysts and the companies that hire them look favorably on certifications, and the general consensus in the industry is that these tools will continue to play a big role in employment decisions for the foreseeable future.

What Skills and Personal Qualities Matter Most— and Why?

Cybersecurity analysts need good analytical and problem-solving skills. They also must be detail oriented, creative, and able to apply what they know about computers and cyberattack mitigation to quickly develop solutions for new challenges. As Steve Morgan puts it, "A knack for cat and mouse play may indicate that you have an aptitude for cybersecurity."[20]

It is also important to have experience with scripting and using computer languages like Python, MySQL, Ruby, and Unix. In many instances analysts must find program bugs that render networks vulnerable or create new security tools, both of which require them to write and analyze code. Indeed, several cybersecurity jobs that were posted in 2016 specified that candidates needed to have experience with JavaScript, Python, and Ruby, along with source code analysis and related skills. "Our lives revolve around code," notes Casaba Security, a consulting firm. "Anyone wishing to work in this field should know how to write code, whether it's scripting, writing native apps, or building Web applications."[21]

An Affinity for Technology

Although analysts can have a variety of academic degrees and backgrounds, they all must share an affinity for technology. "There is no one true path to working in cybersecurity," notes the non-profit organization CyberDegrees.org. "People come at it from all angles—math, computer science, even history or philosophy. Yet all of them share a deep and abiding interest in how technology works." The reason this is so critical is because it is hard to protect something you don't understand. Or, as CyberDegrees.org puts it, "You need to know exactly what you're protecting and the reason things are insecure."[22]

Most analysts have a longtime interest in computers; many learned to program or hack early on. For instance, white-hat hacker Billy Rios figured out how to hack computer games when he was in middle school. One of his first exploits was *Champions of Krynn*; he modified the digital files that save players' moves and game progress (called save game files) to give himself a strategic advantage. "It seems so crazy that hacking save games on 5-1/4 inch disks could set the foundation for a career in cybersecurity,"[23] he says. While a university student in the 1990s, he learned to hack into computer networks. However, he always did this for fun and never tried to steal information or wreak havoc.

> "Our lives revolve around code. Anyone wishing to work in this field should know how to write code, whether it's scripting, writing native apps, or building Web applications."[21]
>
> —Casaba Security consulting firm

In recent years, employers have realized that lifelong computer enthusiasts can make good cybersecurity professionals. The Central Intelligence Agency (CIA), for example, used to retrain its own employees to fill its cybersecurity needs but then got the idea to look for new talent at hacker conventions like Black Hat and DEFCON. "At what age did you take apart the family computer?"[24] asked a CIA table banner at one such convention.

However, most organizations try not to recruit black- or grey-hat (malicious or ethically questionable) hackers. Black hats commit crimes, so they are clearly not good job candidates in most instances. Grey hats are a bit different. Most grey hats want to help defeat the worst types of cybercrime, but they are also willing to use whatever methods are necessary—even illegal ones. "A grey hat often is prepared to break the law through exploiting security network vulnerabilities without prior consent or authorization," explains attorney Cassandra Kirsch, who specializes in Internet and

Cybersecurity analysts must be good problem solvers and have the ability to evaluate and prioritize large amounts of information. They also need to have expertise in many areas of computer technology.

information privacy law. Grey hats operate "on the fringe of civil and criminal liability to report security vulnerabilities."[25] As such, hiring grey hats "requires a level of oversight that is seldom welcomed by the employee or available to the employer,"[26] notes Raef Meeuwisse. Nonetheless, some employers make exceptions, especially in cases involving national security. For instance, in 2016 the FBI hired grey hats to break in to an iPhone belonging to the terrorists responsible for the December 2, 2015, attack on the San Bernardino County Public Health Department that killed fourteen people and injured twenty-two.

Many Paths Lead to Cybersecurity

Raef Meeuwisse is director of the British cybersecurity consulting company Cyber Simplicity Ltd. He is living proof that cybersecurity analysts can possess all kinds of skills and qualities. In fact, his university studies had nothing to do with information technology—he was on a path to become an English teacher, and then decided to pursue a career as an insurance company account manager.

Meeuwisse had a longtime interest in computers and technology, however. "In 1990 I was the only person at university with a mobile phone," he says. He built his first computer in 1994 and went on to teach himself all about computers and information technology. He also has a keen interest in psychology. A self-described extrovert, Meeuwisse especially enjoys understanding what makes people tick. He eventually decided to switch careers and started working for an IT company. He found that his interest in people and good communication skills put him at a distinct advantage, "since most of my colleagues were introvert techies," he notes. Within about eighteen months, Meeuwisse became an IT project manager and gained a reputation for being able to quickly analyze projects and systems. He went on to earn important cybersecurity certifications, designed several important cybersecurity frameworks, and gained experience as a CISO before starting his own company.

Author interview with Raef Meeuwisse, October 27, 2016.

Diverse Skills

While most organizations want to hire ethical individuals, in the field of cybersecurity, doing so can present challenges. Christina Luconi, a human resources officer at Rapid7, which creates cybersecurity analysis tools, notes that "there's a lot of really talented hackers or people with cybersecurity skills—it's finding those folks who want to use their skills for good, not evil."[27]

Another ongoing challenge for hiring managers is finding people with the right balance of hard (technological) and soft (people) skills. Indeed, many experts note that computer "geeks" with excellent hard skills are often introverts who have trouble interacting with others. As data protection and privacy expert Sharon Polsky states, cybersecurity is "not a technology problem; it's a human nature problem. The computers and technology are just tools; it's what people do with (or to) the tools that is the problem."[28] Therefore, the most attractive cybersecurity analyst job applicants know how to develop network defenses based on human as well as technical factors. In some cases the need for a well-rounded analyst may limit the job prospects for an individual who lacks good communication and teamwork skills.

However, many cybersecurity departments are beginning to understand that the best teams are composed of people who have a diverse range of skills that complement each other. Therefore, having a narrower skill set may not necessarily be a problem, so long as the individual has excellent computer skills. "A lot of people see the science in cybersecurity, but the art involved is often misunderstood and under-appreciated," says cybersecurity consultant Jessica Gulick. "Some of the smartest security professionals I know have a background in the arts—in music, painting, literature, or photography. Creative approaches drive innovation and invention in cybersecurity."[29] Others note that teams need a healthy mix of people with technical, communication, business, legal, and negotiation skills.

Still, it is important for every team member to have extensive understanding of both technical and human factors, even if they specialize in a particular area. This is because teams of cybercriminals increasingly include social engineering experts and those well versed in human nature. Consider a well-coordinated APT that occurred in 2011 and involved hackers who were believed to be sponsored by the Chinese government. They used Facebook to learn about people with whom they thought certain

> "Some of the smartest security professionals I know have a background in the arts—in music, painting, literature, or photography. Creative approaches drive innovation and invention in cybersecurity."[29]
>
> —Cybersecurity consultant Jessica Gulick

high-level British military and Ministry of Defence officials would want to associate. They then set up a fake Facebook page for someone they called NATO commander Admiral James Stavridis and tricked the British officials into accepting friend requests from the account. The criminals now had access to these individuals' computers, and they used this access to transmit malware that spread to other computers within the Ministry of Defence network. It not only sought certain types of stored data, but also allowed the hackers to follow computer users' keystrokes and steal personal information. Although no military secrets were exposed, the attack indicated that cybersecurity analysts need to possess social engineering knowledge and skills to match those of the criminals they seek to defeat.

CHAPTER 4

What Is It like to Work as a Cybersecurity Analyst?

Cybersecurity analysts might work for a variety of organizations, including those in health care, manufacturing, financial services, retail, entertainment, national security, law enforcement, computer, and software design. They might also start their own businesses. Some provide in-house security for a particular company as a member of a cybersecurity team, while others are independent consultants hired by various institutions or individuals when needed.

Job Compensation

Specific job duties and salaries vary from employer to employer and depend on the job's location and whether it is in the public or private sector. In general a 2015 study by Burning Glass Technologies Research indicated that cybersecurity professionals' salaries are 9 percent higher than those of other IT professionals. Jobs in large cities and in areas with high costs of living—like Washington, DC, and San Jose, California—pay even more. For example, the average annual salary for an experienced cybersecurity analyst in the United States is approximately $143,000, but the average in Washington, DC, is $160,000.

Private-sector jobs pay significantly more than government jobs, and this factor partially accounts for the disproportionate number of open positions in the government. The average annual salary in the United States for private-sector analysts is $116,000, and upper-level analysts can easily earn $200,000 to $250,000. In comparison, in December 2016 the DHS advertised several positions that paid $92,145 to $141,555 annually, depending on the candidate's experience and job history.

Still, many who work for the government note that exceptional benefits, job training, and job stability make these careers worthwhile. Candidates are also drawn to them because of what CyberDegrees.org calls "Superhero Status"[30]—the fact that government professionals fight drug runners, terrorists, and other extreme (and exciting) threats and are widely regarded as crusaders for the public good. "I have no regrets on my many years working technology infrastructure and cybersecurity jobs at the state and federal level," states Dan Lohrmann, who has worked for the NSA and the Michigan State government. "I was given many, many roles and leadership opportunities as a government official that would not have been possible in the private sector until much later in my career."[31]

A More than Full-Time Job

No matter where a cybersecurity analyst works, most do so full-time—and beyond. The US Department of Labor reports that in 2014, about 25 percent worked more than forty hours per week. Many analysts must also be on call outside normal business hours to attend to emergencies. Security analyst Andrea Hoy is pretty much always on call and says that people who want a job with consistent hours would probably not like working in this field. "My day never really seems to start nor stop," she says. "I tend to 'sleep' with the electronic leash [that is, her phone] by my bed, just in case an incident was to occur."[32] In some companies, after an attack occurs, cybersecurity teams work day and night to troubleshoot, minimize damage, and repair systems. Such companies often provide employees with in-house cafeterias, gyms, and even cots for napping.

> "My day never really seems to start nor stop. I tend to 'sleep' with the electronic leash [that is, her phone] by my bed, just in case an incident was to occur."[32]
>
> —Cybersecurity analyst Andrea Hoy

Some analysts find it stressful to work extended and often inflexible hours. In fact, a 2016 report by the cybersecurity company Alien-Vault revealed that nearly 20 percent of cybersecurity workers considered changing jobs because of the long and strict hours.

Risks to Cybersecurity Analysts

Most cybersecurity analysts do not expect to face criminal charges for researching and exposing digital system weaknesses, but some have indeed encountered this problem. Laws like the Digital Millennium Copyright Act (DMCA) and the Computer Fraud and Abuse Act (CFAA) exist to punish malicious hackers, but sometimes product manufacturers prosecute white-hat hackers for breaking in to their systems. For example, cybersecurity analyst Jay Radcliffe, who has diabetes and uses an insulin pump, first exposed security vulnerabilities in these devices in 2013. He stopped his independent research after being threatened by device manufacturers. Radcliffe then joined the Rapid7 cybersecurity firm as a consultant to investigate vulnerabilities posed by wireless networks in general, which are not subject to criminal prosecution.

Radcliffe and others want lawmakers to amend the DMCA to protect ethical hackers who seek to protect the public. He says that threats made by device manufacturing and hospital representatives and their attorneys have had "a chilling effect" on professionals like himself. Indeed, at a 2014 hospital conference, Partners Healthcare Information Technology administrator Rick Hampton screamed at cybersecurity experts for being troublemakers who create what he called "*National Enquirer* headlines" to incite public hysteria.

Quoted in Kelly Jackson Higgins, "White Hat Hackers Fight for Legal Reform," InformationWeek, Dark Reading, October 21, 2014. www.darkreading.com.

Quoted in Monte Reel and Jordan Robertson, "It's Way Too Easy to Hack the Hospital," *Bloomberg Businessweek*, November 2015. www.bloomberg.com.

The report also noted that many employers found that allowing employees to adopt flexible schedules—for example, letting them work from home one day per week—significantly enhanced their satisfaction and loyalty.

Analysts who work as consultants may need to travel to wherever a client organization is located. Those who specialize in health care institution cybersecurity, for instance, may travel from one hospital to another. Those in some government jobs also travel extensively. The special agents and computer scientists on the FBI's Cyber Action Teams, for example, must be prepared to "travel around the world on a moment's notice to assist in computer intrusion cases [and] gather vital intelligence that helps us identify the cyber crimes that are most dangerous to our national security and to our economy,"[33] the FBI explains. Cyber Action

The Downsides of a Cybersecurity Analysis Job

Cybersecurity analysts earn high salaries and usually like their work. However, many feel stressed from working irregular hours and needing to constantly and quickly adapt to new cyberthreats. They also face the possibility of being blamed for a security breach. Managers find themselves in the position of needing to beg company decision makers to allocate appropriate resources for security. Analysts might be unpopular in their organization, because they are often in the position of having to police other employees' online activities. As security supervisor Tim Pospisil puts it, "We're kind of like the IRS of the organization—no one really likes us."

A 2016 US News survey indicated that compared to other jobs, cybersecurity professionals rated their level of job-related stress as above average. Meanwhile, a 2015 Bureau of Labor Statistics survey revealed that these stressors often lead to health problems such as high blood pressure. Other drawbacks of the job involve health problems that affect anyone who often works with computers—eyestrain, headache, backache, and repetitive motion conditions such as carpal tunnel syndrome, which may involve pain and numbness in the hands and wrists. Doctors recommend that people with such jobs take frequent breaks, practice good posture, do stretching exercises, and perhaps wear wrist splints to help prevent these and similar ailments.

Quoted in Beth Stackpole, "IT Careers: Security Talent Is Red-Hot," *Computerworld*, April 27, 2015. www.computerworld.com.

Teams specialize in analyzing hackers' digital signatures, which are electronic sequences of digits that identify the computer user who sent a particular message. They do so using skills they develop through advanced training in malware analysis, computer languages, and forensics.

Women in Cybersecurity

The often irregular work hours and need for extensive travel contribute to the fact that only 11 percent of cybersecurity professionals are women, according to a 2015 study by the certification organization (ISC)². However, some companies like Hewlett-Packard have implemented more flexible schedules to attract and retain competent female workers who want to better juggle their professional and family obligations. This has helped women like Joy Forsythe, a Hewlett-Packard software security researcher, feel more satisfied with her job. "I can schedule my non-working time during my child's waking hours, and I can come back online after my child goes to bed,"[34] she says.

To address the scarcity of women in the field, numerous organizations have formed that are dedicated to helping women enter and succeed in these jobs. One such group, Women in Cybersecurity, offers information, support, conferences, and scholarships to female cybersecurity analysts. It also works with educational institutions to address the fact that many girls have traditionally avoided STEM-related classes that can open paths to IT jobs.

Indeed, about 90 percent of the students enrolled in American high school computer science classes are boys. "There is a perception that women aren't good at math, science, or technology," states Julie Reeder of (ISC)². "It is this perception that is steering girls away from entering these fields."[35] School officials and teachers are thus encouraging more females to take STEM courses and join cyber clubs and teams.

A Typical Day's Work

The extended hours and travel inherent in many analysts' jobs are not the only factors that create unique challenges in this career field. "This isn't a normal job," says a writer for the Casaba

Security website. "The tasks aren't always clearly defined, and the requirements aren't always known. . . . Our clients depend on us to find the problems that nobody else thought of, and we rely on each other working either individually or as a team, to do the same."[36]

Despite the atypical nature of these jobs, there is still some uniformity to the tasks an analyst may perform on any given day. He or she may do administrative work such as responding to e-mails or preparing reports. Such reports may focus on the status of the organization's digital network or look at whether existing security is effectively blocking or neutralizing threats. The analyst may meet with security department colleagues or managers from other departments to discuss a company's security needs and strategies. Other times, he or she will develop a new security tool or test new software or hardware to ensure it is safe.

On some days an analyst may perform penetration testing or forensically analyze digital clues. Penetration testing may involve breaking in to a computer network using software, or it may require an analyst to physically take apart a digital device, such as a networked smart watch, to examine the electronic components for security weaknesses. Forensic analysis involves preserving and analyzing digital information to uncover and interpret evidence that a criminal may have left about how, where, and when a particular crime occurred. For example, a forensic analyst might examine a hacker's e-mails and Internet browsing history to look for evidence that the hacker planned and committed a particular crime.

> "This isn't a normal job. The tasks aren't always clearly defined, and the requirements aren't always known."[36]
>
> —Casaba Security consulting firm

Staying Updated

No matter what an analyst's precise duties are, cybersecurity analysts must constantly update their knowledge and skills and independently research new threats. This often entails attending industry seminars and conferences and re-qualifying for certifications. "Cybersecurity is not a static discipline that can be learned and applied for years," says Raef Meeuwisse. "An ongoing and substantial personal investment is required to stay on top of the subject area."[37] Meeuwisse speaks from experience—he spends about 20 percent of his time keeping up with new and emerging threats and developments.

Many analysts enjoy the challenge of constantly updating their knowledge and skills. IT security supervisor Tim Pospisil, for instance, states that it "forces you to constantly be on your toes, and it keeps you fresh."[38] However, many find it stressful that the bad guys always seem to be one step ahead—and that some employers do not support the ongoing need to stay current. A 2016 survey by the Information Systems Security Association (ISSA) and the Enterprise Strategy Group noted that 56 percent of cybersecurity employees stated that their employers did not provide the time and training their team needed to stay up-to-date. Nor did they provide enough funding to hire the necessary people or to purchase updated hardware and software. This led these employees to feel "undermanned, underskilled and under-supported."[39] Still, the survey found that 41 percent of cybersecurity professionals are very satisfied with their job; 44 percent are somewhat satisfied, and just 15 percent are not satisfied.

CHAPTER 5

Advancement and Other Job Opportunities

There are a lot of ways in which cybersecurity analysts may advance or be promoted, either within a particular company, by joining another organization, or by starting their own consulting company. However, some advancement paths are more common than others. For example, an entry-level job that involves responding to and analyzing security incidents typically leads to mid-level jobs in penetration testing or in network vulnerability testing.

Advancement comes with new job responsibilities as well as higher salaries. For instance, in December 2016 opening entry-level analyst positions advertised an average annual salary of $70,647. Open mid-level cybersecurity analyst positions, meanwhile, advertised an average of $89,232 per year. (Note that these averages apply only to open jobs; what cybersecurity analysts actually earn once they are working is higher.) In turn, mid-level positions can lead to advanced-level jobs such as cybersecurity managers, administrators, engineers, or architects. In 2016 these open positions were offered at an average salary of $113,407.

The Greatest Needs

While organizations seek analysts at all levels, a 2014 RAND study found it is most difficult to fill upper-level supervisory positions. Indeed, the rapid growth of cybersecurity departments has created a dire need for skilled people to lead them. The main challenge lies in finding knowledgeable, competent IT professionals who also have the leadership, business, and interpersonal skills department leaders need. According to RAND, the most sought-after department leaders, or CISOs, "are those who combine technical talent with business or organizational experience."[40] This is why many CISOs have a combination of academic degrees that encompass IT and business (such as a general MBA or an MBA in cybersecurity), along with several certifications and years of experience.

Raef Meeuwisse describes the CISO role as "the overall manager who has to analyze all the strands of information about an organization's security position, so that they can decipher the priorities and help the management team make informed decisions."[41] Such a role involves suggesting funding and policy changes to boards of directors. In fact, more and more companies with dedicated cybersecurity departments are making CISOs board-level executives. "Everybody speaks business, from the CEO . . . to the other board members. Because of this, it is crucial for the CISO to speak that language too," explains cybersecurity specialist Federico Filacchione. He notes that a CISO's key responsibility is to serve "as a bridge between [the] two worlds"[42] of business and technology.

Billy Rios is an example of someone whose diverse academic degrees and experience prepared him for a leadership role. He

Seminars and conferences, such as this cybersecurity conference in Georgia in 2016, provide a way for cybersecurity analysts to learn about new trends and advances in their field. These events also help analysts create and expand their network of professional contacts.

has a bachelor's degree in business and information systems and master's degrees in business administration, information science, and applied intelligence, along with experience in teaching and as a Marine Corps officer. Together, his academic degrees and work experience helped him advance to positions such as director of vulnerability research and threat intelligence (for the company Qualys) and global managing director of professional services (for Cylance).

Analysts can also pursue specialized certifications for leadership roles. For instance, the GISP (GIAC Information Security Professional) and GSLC (GIAC Security Leadership Certification) specifically train people to move into leadership roles.

Cybersecurity Consultants

Unlike large corporations and government agencies, many smaller companies cannot support an entire in-house cybersecurity staff. Many therefore hire independent consulting firms to meet their needs for specific tasks like penetration testing or dealing with the aftermath and recovery from a cyber breach. Many professionals have started their own consulting companies to meet these needs. A few examples of such companies are root9B, Dell SecureWorks, and FireEye. All employ varying numbers of professionals who excel in a variety of specialties; many also create and sell cybersecurity tools.

Analysts who start their own consulting firms like the opportunity to set their own standards and apply their knowledge to a variety of settings. However, running an independent business is not for everyone, as it requires owners to handle overhead expenses and other business details—including finding work.

"Consultants make recommendations but that doesn't mean companies always listen. This can be a frustrating scenario when you see an organization setting themselves up for problems later."[43]

—CIO.com managing editor Rich Hein

As Rich Hein, managing editor of CIO.com, points out, "You will have a finite amount of time working in any one role." Hein also notes that doing clients' work involves giving up a certain amount

The First Federal Chief Information Security Officer

In September 2016 Brigadier General (retired) Gregory J. Touhill became the first federal CISO. His appointment illustrates the vast potential that qualified cybersecurity analysts have for advancement and promotion. Indeed, a White House press release noted that Touhill was chosen because of his extensive leadership experience and technological knowledge, which he gained from years of working in all different kinds of cybersecurity positions.

Touhill's appointment underscores the federal government's commitment to enhance cybersecurity in the public and private sectors. For example, in 2017 it allocated $19 billion to modernize IT and cybersecurity equipment and to recruit, train, and hire thousands of cybersecurity professionals. Touhill's role in overseeing and coordinating this nationwide initiative places him at the very top of the government hierarchy that seeks to confront and control the growing cybersecurity threats—a role that entails tremendous responsibilities as well as opportunities to influence the course of US history for decades to come.

of control, and some analysts find that difficult. "Consultants make recommendations but that doesn't mean companies always listen," he says. "This can be a frustrating scenario when you see an organization setting themselves up for problems later."[43]

Training and Teaching Professionals

Many analysts who run their own companies or otherwise become authorities on the subject can find work educating other analysts. Teaching opportunities arise at colleges, universities, or technical schools; some also write textbooks and other types of guides for cybersecurity professionals. Some analysts are hired to conduct seminars or give speeches at cybersecurity conferences. One conference that was held in January 2017, for example, featured speakers who were CISOs, CEOs, and senior cybersecurity officials from the US Department of State, the National Institute of Standards and Technology (NIST), and the DHS.

Those who teach and mentor aspiring or rising cybersecurity professionals like the work and find it satisfying. "One of the reasons I enjoy teaching and writing blog posts is to share with you my past mistakes so that you hopefully don't have to suffer through the consequences of those mistakes as I did,"[44] writes Regis University CISO Jonathan Trull.

Paths in Information Technology

Another way to advance in the field of cybersecurity is to transition from a nonsecurity IT career. According to a 2015 report by Burning Glass Technologies, people who already work in IT and switch to an entry-level job in cybersecurity analysis can generally expect to earn 9 percent, or approximately $6,500, more per year than other IT workers.

"One of the reasons I enjoy teaching and writing blog posts is to share with you my past mistakes so that you hopefully don't have to suffer through the consequences of those mistakes as I did."[44]

—Regis University CISO Jonathan Trull

IT professionals who want to switch have a huge advantage because they are already well versed in IT fundamentals. It is possible to make this transition at any point, but the nonprofit organization CyberDegrees.org notes that those who are just beginning a career in IT but anticipate transitioning to cybersecurity later on can make certain choices that make this change easier down the road.

"Think ahead 5–10 years to your ultimate security career, then look for starter IT jobs that will supply you with the right skills,"[45] suggests CyberDegrees.org. For instance, one might work as a network administrator to learn skills to eventually become a cyberforensic analyst or work as a web developer to eventually become a web security analyst. Other IT jobs that can readily lead to a cybersecurity career include computer programmer, software engineer, computer systems analyst, database administrator, IT technician, network engineer, network data analyst, and web administrator.

Another way for IT professionals to transition to a career in cybersecurity is to participate in the FBI's Technically Trained Agent (TTA) program. IT professionals who have a bachelor's degree in computer science, computer engineering, information systems analysis, or technology information management can undergo additional in-house training to move into a career in FBI cybersecurity in one of three specialties. These include becoming a forensic examiner or analyst, who uncovers and analyzes cybercriminals' digital footprints; becoming a threat intelligence analyst, who works with special agents to track down and arrest cybercriminals; or joining a computer analysis response team, which is responsible for similar kinds of tasks.

CHAPTER 6

What Does the Future Hold for Cybersecurity Analysts?

As cybersecurity becomes a central focus for government and private-sector organizations, the need for cybersecurity analysts will grow. The Bureau of Labor Statistics expects job growth in this field to grow 18 percent between 2014 and 2024. This is much higher than the average 6.5 percent growth rate for jobs in general and also exceeds the 12 percent growth rate for other IT jobs.

Organizations have dramatically increased their cybersecurity budgets in response to the growing challenges posed by cyber-crime. These increases will help companies and agencies hire more cybersecurity workers to meet these challenges. For example, in 2015 JPMorgan Chase increased its cybersecurity budget from $250 million to $500 million. Meanwhile, the US government allocated $19 billion for cybersecurity in 2017, compared to $14 billion in 2016.

> "The cybersecurity skills gap is quickly turning into a chasm."[46]
>
> —ISACA chair Christos Dimitriadis

This growing need is made more urgent by an increasing gap between the demand for and supply of eligible job candidates. In October 2016 ISACA reported a dramatic increase in this gap, meaning that the number of available jobs increased much faster than the number of people qualified to fill them. "The cybersecurity skills gap is quickly turning into a chasm,"[46] notes ISACA chair Christos Dimitriadis. A 2016 ISSA survey confirms this demand—it found that 46 percent of information security professionals were solicited at least once per week by employment representatives from various companies.

New IoT Technologies

Experts expect that several trends will fuel the need for cybersecurity analysts. One is the growing number of IoT devices—the more things that are connected to the Internet, the more potential there is for crime. In 2015, EY, a global technology company, issued a report that predicted there will be 50 billion interconnected IoT devices by 2020. The report noted that these devices will increasingly come with features that make them vulnerable to attack. "In a very short time, the IoT will have sensing, analytics and visualization tools, which can be accessed by anyone, anytime and anywhere in the world,"[47] it warned. In addition, IoT devices will increasingly rely on cloud computing, which is vulnerable to hacking.

Security experts have expressed particular concerns about self-driving cars. These vehicles can operate with no human at the controls, and some expect them to completely replace conventional cars in the near future. Like other IoT devices, self-driving cars use Internet-enabled computer systems to control functions that range from braking and acceleration to steering and navigation. While they are a marvel of modern technology and contain numerous safety features, many experts regard them as a security nightmare. In theory a hacker could take control of a car and unlock its doors, disable its heating and cooling system, or even render its brakes and other critical functions useless.

Even with embedded security features to prevent a car being taken over, a 2015 Federal Trade Commission report noted that hackers could gain access to the vast amounts of private information such cars hold about their owners, including their home address, frequent destinations, daily schedule, and driving routines. Clearly, security analysts face numerous challenges on this front.

Machine Learning

Another emerging innovation that poses security challenges is artificial intelligence and machine learning. This type of software educates itself to automatically recognize digital patterns and processes and can learn to block or mimic these patterns. Both cybercriminals and security experts can use these technologies to meet their respective needs.

Advances in self-driving cars and their increasing numbers on the road will likely bring new job opportunities for cybersecurity analysts. Experts believe these vehicles, and their owners, could be vulnerable to attacks by hackers.

For example, criminals are increasingly relying on social engineering to breach digital networks, and machine learning programs can make this easier than ever. One area in which experts foresee that these programs will be useful is in spear-phishing attempts. Spear phishing refers to targeting specific individuals with phishing communications, rather than simply sending out millions of identical phishing messages. Thus, a hacker might look at a target's social media accounts to find out about the individual. If the person likes to hang out at Starbucks, the hacker might send a spear-phishing e-mail disguised as a coupon for $10 off a Starbucks purchase. If the link the victim opens contains a machine learning program, the software can then monitor the person's e-mails, web browsing, and phone conversations. It could even learn to mimic this individual's writing and speaking habits.

In the end, hackers could use this data to generate spear-phishing e-mails or text messages that genuinely appear to be composed and sent by the victim to friends on the victim's contact list. As Dave Palmer, technology director at the cybersecurity company Darktrace, points out, "It's come from me, it sounds like me, it talks about the things we usually talk about. I expect they'd open it."[48] This way, hackers can easily increase their victim population. Jonathan Sander of the Lieberman Software security management company discusses another way in which hackers might use machine learning software. "Imagine if it could even text us and pretend to be our kid asking for the Netflix password because they forgot it,"[49] he states.

However, machine learning has also offered cybersecurity analysts new ways to fight back. For example, a program called Mayhem, developed by the Pittsburgh-based company ForAllSecure, combines a system that searches for computer code flaws with one that develops patches, or fixes, for these flaws. This helps analysts by speeding up the process of detecting and developing ways to fix the vulnerabilities that hackers exploit. Experts believe this will allow cybersecurity professionals to keep up with the ways in which hackers continuously modify malware so it escapes detection. As DARPA (the US government's Defense Advanced Research Projects Agency, which studies technologies that can be used in national defense) program manager Mike Walker states, innovations like this "will speed the day when networked attackers no longer have the inherent advantage they have now."[50]

Another new product is Allure Security's Novo, which combines machine learning with what the company calls decoy technology. Novo analyzes and responds to unusual data patterns and to changes in individual users' online behavior. If a particular company employee usually logs on to his computer in Chicago, for example, and suddenly appears to log in from India, the software will alert security people that the individual's computer may have been hacked. This will help security professionals protect organizations against outsider and insider threats. Allure Security explains that Novo "continuously learns as you do. Novo adapts to how you work . . . it acts to protect devices if it notices something weird happening and offers prioritized alerts in real time so security pros can check out anything unusual."[51]

Although such systems can work independently, experts like ForAllSecure CEO David Brumley note that these technologies will not replace people who work in cybersecurity. "I look at computers freeing us from mundane tasks," he states. "You always want that spark of human creativity, and that's something the computer will never have."[52]

A New Type of Warfare

Cyberattacks are increasingly directed at government and institutional computer networks and therefore constitute a new type of warfare. Indeed, hackers known as hacktivists—those who have political motivations—have already shut down or done significant damage to entire countries.

The most damaging intrusion to date occurred in April 2007, when Russian hacktivists became upset after the country Estonia moved a statue honoring Russian soldiers who fought in World War II. In response, they flooded Estonia's government, communications, and financial websites with cybertraffic. They also infected millions of computers with malware that together created a botnet, which also participated in the attack. Websites that were equipped to receive a thousand visits per day crashed after being overwhelmed with two thousand visits per minute. The attack shut down the Estonian government and economy.

The Estonian government considered the attack to be an act of war and believes the Russian government orchestrated it (though this has not been proven). As Estonian defense minister Jaak Aaviksoo puts it, the attack "can effectively be compared to when your ports are shut to the sea."[53] Some national security experts have suggested that Russia may have chosen to attack via cyberspace because it was a safer way to inflict damage. Had Russia, say, bombed or invaded Estonia, it would have triggered a military response from the North Atlantic Treaty Organization (NATO), with which Estonia is aligned. But cyberattacks tend to be untraceable, which makes them harder to respond to. As national security expert Stephen Herzog explains, "Russia cannot risk attacks on NATO member states, perhaps making unattributable cyber strikes an attractive alternative."[54]

National security experts are also worried about cyberattacks on critical computerized infrastructure components, which include power grids, air traffic controls, and military weapons systems.

A Place for Biologists in Cybersecurity?

Most cybersecurity experts have degrees and experience in information technology. But those with a background in biology might also have a future in this field. In 2016 a biomedical engineer named Lalit Mestha led a research project to build cybersecurity systems that are modeled on how the human body combats unwanted intruders like viruses. The body's immune system uses a variety of cells and chemicals to identify and fight such invaders. Mestha and other researchers hope to adapt these mechanisms to computers in a way that will help them detect and respond to cyberattacks.

Some computers already contain sensors that detect such attacks, but researchers hope to refine them to make them more like biological detection mechanisms that launch specific defenses for different types of attacks. "We want to . . . enable the machine to adjust its operation in response to an attack just like the human body does to pathogen attacks or infections," Mestha explains. This type of approach is intended to augment other layers of cybersecurity, including anti-malware tools and access controls. Mestha's emerging field of research indicates there may be opportunities for medical doctors to work on cybersecurity teams to create such systems.

Quoted in Todd Alhart, "These Scientists Are Hacking the Immune System to Fight Hackers," GE Reports, December 2, 2016. www.gereports.com.

This concern was heightened in 2010, when foreign hackers used malware called Stuxnet to disable Iranian nuclear centrifuges. Unlike most malware, which aims to do widespread damage, Stuxnet was engineered to harm computers with specific configurations. It was thus used like a "smart bomb" to achieve a specific objective. Attacks on infrastructure have taken place in other countries, too—for example, in Ukraine in 2015, when foreign hackers disrupted the nation's electric power grid.

Cyberwarfare will influence the directions in which cybersecurity jobs evolve in the future. In fact, after the Estonia attack, world leaders realized that cyberattacks require strategic planning and cooperation among nations, just like traditional war readiness does. Cybersecurity experts from Germany, Finland, Slovenia, Israel, and NATO nations all helped the Estonian government's Computer Emergency Response Team restore operations. Other worldwide strategic planning and response networks were set up to address future cyberwarfare attacks.

"We are only at the dawn of cybersecurity. Things are going to get worse before they get better."[55]

—Cyber Simplicity Ltd. director Raef Meeuwisse

Existing challenges and emerging trends will shape the future of cybersecurity careers. While there is debate over which methods will best address the threats, it is clear that there will be an ongoing and growing need for cybersecurity professionals in the future. "We are only at the dawn of cybersecurity," notes Raef Meeuwisse. "Things are going to get worse before they get better."[55]

CHAPTER 7

Interview with a Cybersecurity Analyst

Billy Rios is a cybersecurity analyst affiliated with the WhiteScope company, which he founded. He has worked in cybersecurity since 2004 and has expertise in developing cybersecurity systems, performing penetration testing, analyzing and mitigating security threats, conducting forensics, and leading and training cybersecurity teams. He is widely known for his work in exposing vulnerabilities in electronic medical devices, aircraft, and military weapons systems. Rios has also received numerous awards and citations for assisting the Department of Homeland Security's ICS Cyber Emergency Response Team. He spoke with the author about his career via e-mail.

Q: Why did you become a cybersecurity analyst?

A: I've been tinkering with cybersecurity since I was in middle school. One of the first "cybersecurity" projects I worked on was hacking video games to modify the high scores list and access special weapons within the game. I didn't realize that learning how to modify the game was actually hands-on learning about how computers really worked. By hacking computer games, I learned how computer processors execute instructions, how memory works, how the file systems are structured, how to run time dependencies, and even how copy software protection works. These lessons were the foundation for the career I have today.

Q: Can you describe your typical workday?

A: I wake up and make my bed (a positive habit learned in the Marine Corps). Usually I spend a few minutes thinking through priorities for the day. I try to work on the stuff I hate most in the morning. This is usually paperwork or administrative work that every business needs to do. Then I work on something technical, whether it's taking apart an embedded device, doing vulnerability research, or writing code. I try to do something technical every day. It's surprising how quickly technical skills can atrophy if they are not exercised. I have a family, so I allocate time to spend with the family. At night, I work on things that didn't get done during the day.

Q: What personal qualities do you find most valuable for people in this type of work?

A: Persistence and initiative. I've had the opportunity to work with a number of extremely talented people in the industry. I've seen that most of the folks who can take it to the next level have a tenacious persistence that drives them to understand the problem sets and solutions they are facing. Also, many of the problems we face don't have straightforward solutions. Taking the initiative to learn about things and try things is important. If you want someone to hand hold you through these processes, you probably won't get very far.

Q: How did your military career prepare you for your present line of work?

A: Many folks don't know this, but I was an active duty Marine Corps officer who served in Operation Iraqi Freedom in 2003. The Marine Corps thrives on persistence and initiative. It's something that is instilled in Marines through all levels of training and in all military specialties. Working with the signals intelligence folks didn't hurt either.

Q: What do you like most about your job?

A: It's challenging. After spending most of my adult life in cybersecurity, it's still really, really challenging. There are still nights where I literally can't sleep because I'm compelled to figure out how something works. While the foundation I've built over the last few decades allows me to quickly dissect complex systems, it seems like every system has parts that are unique.

Q: What do you like least about your job?

A: There is a lot of work that's needed in order to properly run a business (marketing, business development, legal, and regular admin). I've learned a lot about how businesses are run, and it's an important skill set to build, but I've never had a passion for it.

Q: What advice do you have for students who might be interested in pursuing a career in cybersecurity analysis?

A: Foundational knowledge is important. Don't worry about specific tools and techniques—those will inevitably change over time. Learn the foundations of how computers, software, and networking work. If you know these areas really well, you'll be able to learn the rest quickly. Pick an area that you like and go for it! There are numerous specialties within cybersecurity, all of which require different mind-sets and skills. No one area is "better" than another. If you find yourself drawn to vulnerability research, then go for it! If you like incident response, go for it! It's also okay to switch. If you find yourself getting bored with your current research projects, try working with someone in a different cybersecurity discipline.

Q: What factors do you think are important to consider in the growing need for cybersecurity analysts?

A: Building the workforce is the most difficult problem we face in cybersecurity. I always cringe when I hear someone say, "It's so easy—you can just watch a YouTube video and learn how to hack XYZ." Learning how to use a tool is completely different than learning cybersecurity—both offense and defense. Many of the situations we face are complex and take a deep understanding of how systems work. Throw in the usual mix of politics, administration, and logistics, and you quickly find that doing real work in cybersecurity is more than watching a few YouTube videos. Given the steep learning curve and the requisite investment required in training someone to be a "journeyman" or "expert" cybersecurity professional, this is a problem we'll be facing for the foreseeable future.

SOURCE NOTES

Introduction: The Need for Cybersecurity Analysts

1. P.W. Singer and Allan Friedman, *Cybersecurity and Cyberwar*. New York: Oxford University Press, 2014, p. 2.
2. James B. Comey, "FBI Budget Request for Fiscal Year 2017," Statement Before the House Appropriations Committee, Subcommittee on Commerce, Justice, Science, and Related Agencies, Washington, DC, February 25, 2016. www.fbi.gov.
3. Quoted in Nena Giandomenico and Juliana de Groot, "Insider vs. Outsider Data Security Threats: What's the Greater Risk?," *Digital Guardian* (blog), October 14, 2016. https://digitalguardian.com.
4. Comey, "FBI Budget Request for Fiscal Year 2017."
5. Tony Scott and J. Michael Daniel, "Announcing the First Federal Chief Information Security Officer," *The White House Blog*, September 8, 2016. https://obamawhitehouse.archives.gov.

Chapter One: What Does a Cybersecurity Analyst Do?

6. Kirk Steinklauber, "Data Security Defense in Depth: The Onion Approach to IT Security," SecurityIntelligence, January 15, 2015. https://securityintelligence.com.
7. Quoted in ISACA, "CSX North America Conference Report," October 26, 2016. www.isaca.org.
8. Quoted in Drew Harwell, "Russian Hackers Keep Business Booming for Irvine Cybersecurity Firm," *Los Angeles Times*, August 2, 2016. www.latimes.com.
9. Author interview with Raef Meeuwisse, October 27, 2016.

Chapter Two: How Do You Become a Cybersecurity Analyst?

10. Quoted in Joe Napsha, "Norwin IUP, FBI Team Up for Model Cyber Security Program," *TribLive*, January 27, 2016. www.triblive.com.
11. Quoted in Lauren Loricchio, "Catonsville High Cyber Team Members Prepare for the Future," *Baltimore Sun*, October 28, 2014. www.baltimoresun.com.
12. Quoted in SANS Institute, "GIAC Launches New Certification for Python Coders, GPYC," May 9, 2016. www.sans.org.
13. Quoted in Global Information Assurance Certification, "Certifications: Why Certify?," www.giac.org.
14. Quoted in Global Information Assurance Certification, "Certifications: Why Certify?"

15. Quoted in ISACA, "What CISMs Are Saying." www.isaca.org.
16. Quoted in ISACA, "What CISMs Are Saying."
17. Steve Morgan, "One Million Cybersecurity Job Openings in 2016," *Forbes*, January 2, 2016. www.forbes.com.
18. Author interview with Billy Rios, December 7, 2016.
19. National Research Council of the National Academies, *Professionalizing the Nation's Cybersecurity Workforce?* Washington, DC: National Academies Press, 2013, p. 19.

Chapter Three: What Skills and Personal Qualities Matter Most—and Why?

20. Morgan, "One Million Cybersecurity Job Openings in 2016."
21. Casaba Security, "Jobs." www.casaba.com.
22. CyberDegrees.org, "Career Path Options." www.cyberdegrees.org.
23. Quoted in Pierluigi Paganini, "Hacker Interviews—Billy Rios," Security Affairs, July 5, 2016. http://securityaffairs.co.
24. Quoted in Martin C. Libicki, David Senty, and Julia Pollak, "Hackers Wanted: An Examination of the Cybersecurity Labor Market," RAND National Security Research Division, 2014. www.rand.org.
25. Cassandra Kirsch, "Grey Hat Hacking: Reconciling Law with Cyber Reality," *Northern Kentucky Law Review*, vol. 41, no. 3, 2014, pp. 386, 388.
26. Raef Meeuwisse, *Cybersecurity Exposed: The Cyber House Rules*. Hythe, Kent, UK: Cyber Simplicity Ltd., 2017, p. 143.
27. Quoted in Sandrine Rastello and Jeanna Smialek, "Cybersecurity Starts in High School with Tomorrow's Hires," *Bloomberg Technology*, May 15, 2013. www.bloomberg.com.
28. Quoted in Giandomenico and de Groot, "Insider vs. Outsider Data Security Threats."
29. Quoted in Kathleen Smith, "Cybersecurity Is More than Technical Skills," *Inside the Net* (blog), April 4, 2015. http://blog.clearedjobs.net.

Chapter Four: What Is It like to Work as a Cybersecurity Analyst?

30. CyberDegrees.org, "Government Cyber Security Careers." www.cyberdegrees.org.
31. Dan Lohrmann, "The Case for Taking a Government Cyber Job: 7 Recommendations to Consider," CSO, August 7, 2014. www.csoonline.com.
32. Quoted in *U.S. News & World Report*, "Information Security Analyst," 2016. www.money.usnews.com.
33. Federal Bureau of Investigation, "Cyber Crime." www.fbi.gov.
34. Quoted in Maria Korolov, "Info Sec Industry Still Struggles to Attract Women," CSO, March 25, 2014. www.csoonline.com.
35. Quoted in Korolov, "Info Sec Industry Still Struggles to Attract Women."
36. Casaba Security, "Jobs."

37. Raef Meeuwisse, *Cybersecurity for Beginners*. Canterbury, Kent, UK: Cyber Simplicity Ltd., 2015, p. 56.
38. Quoted in Beth Stackpole, "IT Careers: Security Talent Is Red-Hot," *Computerworld*, April 27, 2015. www.computerworld.com.
39. Quoted in Enterprise Strategy Group and Information Systems Security Association, "ESG and ISSA Research Reveals Cyber Security Profession at Risk," October 5, 2016. www.issa.org.

Chapter Five: Advancement and Other Job Opportunities

40. Libicki et al., "Hackers Wanted."
41. Meeuwisse interview.
42. Federico Filacchione, "The CISO and the Need for a Common Business Language," Security Intelligence, February 2, 2015. https://securityintelligence.com.
43. Rich Hein, "IT Consulting: Is Moving Out on Your Own the Right Move?," CIO.com, April 20, 2015. www.cio.com.
44. Jonathan Trull, "Security Awareness," *Information Assurance* (blog). www.informationassurance.regis.edu.
45. CyberDegrees.org, "Career Path Options."

Chapter Six: What Does the Future Hold for Cybersecurity Analysts?

46. Quoted in ISACA, "New Cybersecurity Jobs Index from ISACA Shows Skills Gap Is Growing," October 13, 2016. www.isaca.org.
47. EY, "Cybersecurity and the Internet of Things," March 2015. www.ey.com.
48. Quoted in Danny Palmer, "How AI-Powered Cyberattacks Will Make Fighting Hackers Even Harder," ZDNet, December 14, 2016. www.zdnet.com.
49. Quoted in Palmer, "How AI-Powered Cyberattacks Will Make Fighting Hackers Even Harder."
50. Quoted in Sharon Gaudin, "'Mayhem' Takes First in DARPA's All-Computer Hacking Challenge," ITWorld, August 5, 2016. www.itworld.com.
51. Allure Security, "Novo." www.alluresecurity.com.
52. Quoted in Gaudin, "'Mayhem' Takes First in DARPA's All-Computer Hacking Challenge."
53. Quoted in Stephen Herzog, "Revisiting the Estonian Cyber Attacks: Digital Threats and Multinational Responses," *Journal of Strategic Security*, vol. 4, no. 2, Summer 2011, p. 54.
54. Herzog, "Revisiting the Estonian Cyber Attacks: Digital Threats and Multinational Responses," p. 53.
55. Meeuwisse, *Cybersecurity for Beginners*, p. xvi.

Cyberdegrees.org

1133 Fifteenth St. NW, 12th Floor
Washington, DC 20005
website: www.cyberdegrees.org

Cyberdegrees.org is a Washington, DC–based nonprofit organization that provides detailed information about existing and emerging government cybersecurity careers. It offers a directory of colleges, universities, and online courses that lead to cybersecurity degrees, information on cybersecurity career paths, cybersecurity certifications, government security clearances, and guidance on how to transition from general information technology careers to specific cybersecurity careers.

Cyber Seek

website: http://cyberseek.org

Cyber Seek is a website designed for employers, career counselors, students, policy makers, and current cybersecurity professionals who are interested in cybersecurity jobs. The website provides detailed, up-to-date information on cybersecurity job opportunities in various places, along with career path, salary, and certification information.

International Information Systems Security Certification Consortium (ISC)[2]

(ISC)[2] Americas
311 Park Place Blvd., Suite 400
Clearwater, FL 33759
website: www.isc2.org

(ISC)[2] is an international nonprofit organization that offers training and certifications for cybersecurity professionals. It also educates the public about security issues and sponsors scholarships and research on security topics.

ISACA

3701 Algonquin Rd., Suite 1010
Rolling Meadows, IL 60008
website: www.isaca.org

The ISACA is an independent nonprofit international organization that provides information, guidance, and opportunities to obtain professional certifications for people in cybersecurity and information systems jobs. Its website also provides information about what cybersecurity jobs involve and what employers are looking for.

National Institute for Cybersecurity Education (NICE)

website: www.csrc.nist.gov

NICE is a national initiative led by the National Institute of Standards and Technology (NIST), which offers detailed information about cybersecurity education, training, and work opportunities for students and others interested in cybersecurity jobs.

SANS Institute

8120 Woodmont Ave., Suite 310
Bethesda, MD 20814
website: www.sans.org

The SANS Institute is a college and professional cybersecurity training school that trains cybersecurity professionals worldwide. It also provides information about cybersecurity itself and about the certifications and training needed for certain cybersecurity jobs. SANS runs the Internet Storm Center, which serves as the Internet's early warning system for announcing cyber threats and attacks.

INDEX

ABOUT THE AUTHOR

Melissa Abramovitz is an award-winning freelance writer/author who specializes in writing educational nonfiction books and magazine articles for all age groups, from preschoolers through adults. She also writes short stories, poems, and picture books and is the author of a book for writers. Abramovitz graduated summa cum laude from the University of California, San Diego, with a degree in psychology. She is also a graduate of the Institute of Children's Literature.